The Land in the Jar

Crofton Infant School
Towncourt Lane
Petts Wood, BR5 1EL

PHASE 3

/igh/ar/

Level 4 – Blue

Helpful Hints for Reading at Home

The graphemes (written letters) and phonemes (units of sound) used throughout this series are aligned with Letters and Sounds. This offers a consistent approach to learning whether reading at home or in the classroom.

HERE IS A LIST OF NEW GRAPHEMES FOR THIS PHASE OF LEARNING. AN EXAMPLE OF THE PRONUNCIATION CAN BE FOUND IN BRACKETS.

Phase 3			
j (jug)	v (van)	w (wet)	x (fox)
y (yellow)	z (zoo)	zz (buzz)	qu (quick)
ch (chip)	sh (shop)	th (thin/then)	ng (ring)
ai (rain)	ee (feet)	igh (night)	oa (boat)
oo (boot/look)	ar (farm)	or (for)	ur (hurt)
ow (cow)	oi (coin)	ear (dear)	air (fair)
ure (sure)	er (corner)		

HERE ARE SOME WORDS WHICH YOUR CHILD MAY FIND TRICKY.

Phase 3 Tricky Words			
he	you	she	they
we	all	me	are
be	my	was	her

GPC focus: /igh/ar/

TOP TIPS FOR HELPING YOUR CHILD TO READ:

- Allow children time to break down unfamiliar words into units of sound and then encourage children to string these sounds together to create the word.
- Encourage your child to point out any focus phonics when they are used.
- Read through the book more than once to grow confidence.
- Ask simple questions about the text to assess understanding.
- Encourage children to use illustrations as prompts.

This book focuses on the phonemes /igh/ and /ar/ and is a blue level 4 book band.

The Land in the Jar

Written by
Emilie Dufresne

Illustrated by
Maia Batumashvili

Carlee had a project to do. She had to hand it in that week.

She had a think. Then she had a plan.

Carlee took a look at her sandwich and put it in the jar.

She did the jar up tight and put in a vent.

Carlee took the jar with her to the park.

She took it to bed at night and held it tight to her.

She took it to the yard. "Carlee, the rain!"

The jar sat in the rain. Boom! Lightning hit the jar.

The jar sat in the yard that night.
Carlee did not go back for the jar.

Carlee had to hand it in.
"We must go, Carlee."

"The jar!"
Carlee ran to the yard and took a look.

Carlee had a look. It had to win!

She ran right back in to get a good look.

"That is odd!" Was that… No… Was it?

The jar had a tree and a kid and a car!
It was such a sight!

The jar! All of this in the jar!

She took a look at a man with a bell on his arm.

He was mad. His arm shot high up.
Carlee took a look.

"Carlee, if we do not get a lot of jars, we will go."

"We need a big jar – a lot of jars! Or we will all go when Miss Tarn has a look!"

"If we go, you will not win. Will you get us a lot of jars, Carlee?"

"A lot of jars – all right. I will get you all the jars."

Carlee took the jar in. Miss Tarn got up.
"… and the thing that will win is…"

"… this jar, Carlee!"
Carlee took a look in the jar.

That week she got ten jars. She took all the jars up to her room.

Soon Carlee's room was all jars and they did not fit in her room.

The Land in the Jar

1. What did Carlee put in her jar at the beginning of the story?

2. Where did Carlee take the jar to?

3. What did the man have on his arm?

    (a) A jar

    (b) A horn

    (c) A bell

4. How many jars did Carlee get?

5. Why was the man angry? How did Carlee make him feel better?

©2021 **BookLife Publishing Ltd.**
King's Lynn, Norfolk PE30 4LS

ISBN 978-1-83927-396-4

All rights reserved. Printed in Malaysia.
A catalogue record for this book is available from the British Library.

The Land in the Jar
Written by Emilie Dufresne
Illustrated by Maia Batumashvili

An Introduction to BookLife Readers...

Our Readers have been specifically created in line with the London Institute of Education's approach to book banding and are phonetically decodable and ordered to support each phase of Letters and Sounds.

Each book has been created to provide the best possible reading and learning experience. Our aim is to share our love of books with children, providing both emerging readers and prolific page-turners with beautiful books that are guaranteed to provoke interest and learning, regardless of ability.

BOOK BAND GRADED using the Institute of Education's approach to levelling.

PHONETICALLY DECODABLE supporting each phase of Letters and Sounds.

EXERCISES AND QUESTIONS to offer reinforcement and to ascertain comprehension.

BEAUTIFULLY ILLUSTRATED to inspire and provoke engagement, providing a variety of styles for the reader to enjoy whilst reading through the series.

> **AUTHOR INSIGHT:**
> **EMILIE DUFRESNE**
>
> Born in Québec, Canada, Emilie Dufresne's academic achievements explain the knowledge and creativity that can be found in her books. At a young age, she received the award of Norfolk County Scholar, recognising her top grades in school. At the University of Kent, Emilie obtained a First Class Honours degree in English and American Literature, and was awarded a Masters in The Contemporary with Distinction. She has published over 60 books with BookLife Publishing, in subjects ranging from science to geography, art and sports, and even animals as superheroes! Children enjoy Emilie's books because of the detailed narrative and the engaging way she writes, which always entices children to want to learn more.

This book focuses on the phonemes /igh/ and /ar/ and is a blue level 4 book band.